21 Years

Brittany Pleiman

BookLeaf Publishing

Presentation by *BookLeaf Publishing*

Web: www.bookleafpub.com

E-mail: info@bookleafpub.com

ISBN: 9789358368192

First edition 2023

For Mrs. Gray,

*I will return to school someday, but for now, I
will go forth and do good things.*

ACKNOWLEDGEMENT

I'm delusional enough to believe that the people in my life whom I'm thankful for already know I feel this way, but just in case, I have a few people I'd like to acknowledge.

Meghan, thank you for always making an effort with me and supporting me from the sidelines, even when it's been difficult for you. You've inspired more than a few poems, and I know at least one made it into this collection.

Ryann, thank you for experiencing every part of life with me. Learning, growing, and living with you and Ashton has already changed and inspired me in more ways than I can count. You are my rock.

Amanda, thank you for approaching every bit of life with such enthusiasm. You've never failed to put a smile on my face, encourage me, or drop everything to help me when I need you. You are sunshine incarnate, and you take amazing photos.

Courtney, thank you for making me feel like I can do anything, and also for teaching me the skills to make anything happen.

Mason, thank you for the endless care you give me, the unending patience, and for not getting irritated when I ask you to be quiet for a moment so that I can write down a word or a phrase. You take care of me when I forget to do so myself, and that's what makes something like this possible. Thank you for the endless encouragement and praise. Without it, I would've quit writing long before anything like this could happen.

Niyah, thank you for being my lifeline, for always giving honest feedback (no matter how much it hurts), and for providing me with over ten years of inspiration. You are the cause of so many of the poems in this collection.

I would also like to thank the incredible BookLeaf team for helping me make this not just possible, but exactly the way I always dreamed it would be.

And finally, I'd like to thank every single person who has ever come into or out of my life. Every interaction has come together to create me and has therefore created this collection.

If you've made it this far, thank you.

PREFACE

Writing is easy, but letting the world in to read that writing is terrifying, and I've always avoided it. Allowing others to read my writing means that I am giving them a part of myself; I am giving them my mind and my heart, and I'm showing them exactly how these two organs work together to create me. It's scary, stripping yourself so bare in front of others, but there's not much we can accomplish if we refuse to interact with fear.

I've spent my life writing everywhere I can: my laptop, my arms, bathroom walls, napkins, scraps of paper ripped from day planners, and in the margins of tests that need to be handed in to the professor in fifteen minutes. I've spent my life writing every time I can: in meetings, in class, during dates and dinners, while flying between states, and while getting tattoos. And I've spent my life writing during every version of myself: every age, every personality difference, every hair color, every partner, every friend group, every university, every mistake, and every experience. And finally, after all of these years and all of this life, I feel ready to share.

This is what it has all come to.

21 Years of me.

Dunewood Drive

I used to love that old Weeping Willow
that stood guard at the end of the cul-de-sac,
blocking the swamp from peering into our
suburbia.
He did his job well, but we did not ask for his
protection.
I will never forget the mouse that my mother
rolled out of our garage with her old, ratty
broom,
or the simple garden snake that my father
picked up like a ramen noodle between
two long branches and cast back into the swamp,
as if the snake had not been borrowing the earth
the same as us.
Nor will I forget the burrs--
oh, the burrs, stuck to our socks,
our shirts, the tops of our tennis shoes,
clinging to us in search of a second life
as we made our way home for dinner.
I must mention the dead tree in our backyard,
right at the edge of the swamp.
He was hunched over, beaten by time,
peeling and decrepit, naked of bark in his
weathered age.
In the winter, when my sled sent me careening

right into his ankles,
I shrieked and cried and panicked.
When I finally thrashed my way out of his
limp, reaching arms, I ran as far away from him
as I could,
covered in scratches from his twisting thorns.
I did not go near that part of the swamp again.
I suppose he did a better job of protecting me
than anyone else ever has.

Life Lesson #1

My father always told me,
"You are always either growing or dying."
But how fickle this weather must be
for me to be in full summer bloom on Monday,
and to fade to a brown shriveled stem by
Wednesday.
I often forget
what exactly it means to grow.
To be growing.
Growth is a process.
An evolution.
A long, enduring period of time,
with little result.
And while watering my cactus today,
my cactus, with its yellowing, decaying body
and a robust pink flower on top,
I realized that even while dying,
there is still growth to be found.

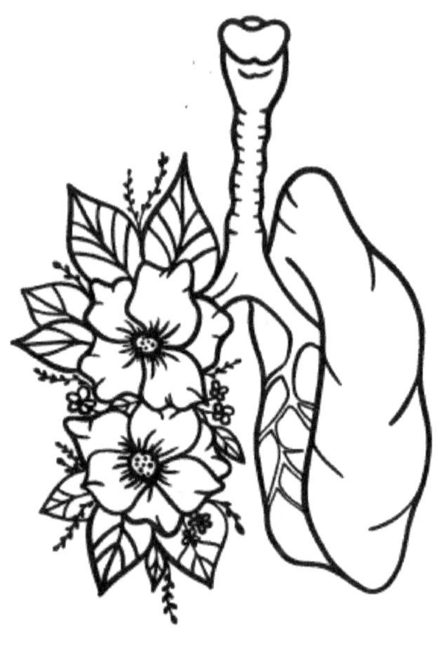

Envy

A golden radiance,
as sweet as the whisper between
blades of grass,
drips from her touch like the trickle
of rain into a long-forgotten
creek.

I would shudder as her
silent ghost passes through me if
not for the sugary warmth,
so like that of the mortals', replacing my
sense.

If only striking a
match upon one's soul could be
the same as lighting up a room,
we would all be gods among
men.

Anxiety

I am stuck in my own lungs.
I am the air.
And I cannot figure out
how to get out--
probably because I am not
supposed
to be air.
I hear the heart galloping
like a stampede of bulls,
another thing I am not
supposed
to be.
So many rules!
Everything set in stone!
I am--who knows what?
But I am not these things.
At least that's a fact I can
remember.
But I cannot remember how to
get out.
This is where it ends.

Obsessive-Compulsive

Tik, tik, tik, tik,
like a metronome,
or like pinpricks of rain on your windshield
as you go 85 on the interstate.
You cannot stop them from coming.
Their hands will beat on the glass until it
shatters.
They will come in.
You will give in.
Clipboard, clipboard, clipboard, clipboard.
Say it four times, then three,
then another ten,
then until you get to twenty-three.
If that's not enough, go on to fifty-six.
It will not end.
Tik, tik, tik, tik.
You will simply board up the windows.
(You will never have time to replace the glass.
They'll be back before then.)
Sigh at yourself. Go back to what you were
doing.
Pretend you're not frustrated with yourself,
with the mind you cannot always control.
Wait for it.
Tik, tik, tik, tik.

Levels (Free Association)

Contemplate. Regenerate. Where's my high?
Thought I had it. Reality? Who is that?
Ink my skin. Will it kill my soul? Old school.
No worries around here.
It won't send. Take me away.
A train is coming.
It's shaking the world.
I am the world. I am shaking.
Eerie.
It's over. We can't die without life.
Is that it? There's my high.
I'm going up.

And coming down. What's underground?
We assume. No questions.
I could be. We are.
Is it always this dark?
Cleanse. Repeat. Cleanse.
Stop. How?
The road is broken.
Let's go back up.

Too high. Life is back.
I see it all.
Trade it. I don't need it.
Sharpen the edges. Come into focus.
Answer the phone.
Where did the darkness go?
My hands are tied.
Answer the goddamn phone.
Damned. The ink is seeping.
Step quietly.
We are not here.
We are not here.

Flip the switch. Too much skin.
Nail polish heart. Chipped.
Don't listen. Hear.
We are one.
The ground is made for us.
Hit it. Nonsense.
Speak from reason.
Voices. We don't need them.
Hit it. Are we stuck?
I want to fly.
Hit it. I'm alone.
We can go.

Up. It burns.
It loves me.
Unconscious. Ink me.
Don't let me leave.
Ruin. Ruin. Stained.
Breathe out.
We are gone.
I am here.
Chains. Wings.
They're the same.
I am free.
Don't let me leave.
I am alone.

I will not leave.

Snakes

I am scared of spiders and paranormal movies,
the thought of my dogs being hit by a car or
my sister or my mother dying.
I am scared of ordering my own food at a
drive-thru,
being fired from a job again, and of tsunami-
sized waves rising over me.
I am scared of speaking and not speaking,
of existing only in ink on pages, being
interpreted
in a way I don't mean.
I am scared of being alone, for a second and a
lifetime,
scared of finding out who I'd be left with
if I only had myself.
I am scared of being too much for everyone and
scared of not being enough for myself. Flip
it around and I'm scared of that too.
Of killing my plants--my cacti, my bonsai,
my hibiscus--and of wasting my life for no
particular reason, I am scared.
Of needles, the kind that give shots and
draw blood, and of ruining other people's lives
without knowing it, I am scared.
But I am not scared of snakes.

Desperation

I'm throwing rocks against God's window,
wondering if there is anyone left to open it
and stick their head out.
They're pebbles--just pebbles, you understand?--
that I'm throwing.
The little pattering they make against the glass
could be an answer,
could be whispered suggestions.
("Try the back door; it's unlocked.")
But it's not what I'm looking for.
It's not "what" I'm looking for.
It's not even "who" I'm looking for.
It's one in the morning and the grass
Is dewy around my ankles and
I have a handful of pebbles cradled in my palm.
For the life of me, I have no idea why.

For Rent

"Face your fears" they always say,
so I turn to the mirror.
I am a stranger to myself.
It's ironic.
I've grown up with myself,
known myself for at least my whole life,
yet I am a vacancy.
Strangers stay in me, from time to time,
sometimes for months on end,
and sometimes they feel familiar.
They never stay,
at least not forever.
So I chase the youth.
I am the youth.
I chase myself,
the myself I would have been,
the myself that I was for a second.
I've been so many selves,
too many to count, surely.
Sometimes I get the feeling that
I am the imposter among them,
rather than the landlord they all have in
common.
Sometimes I get the feeling that
I am not the only one looking
out of these eyes.

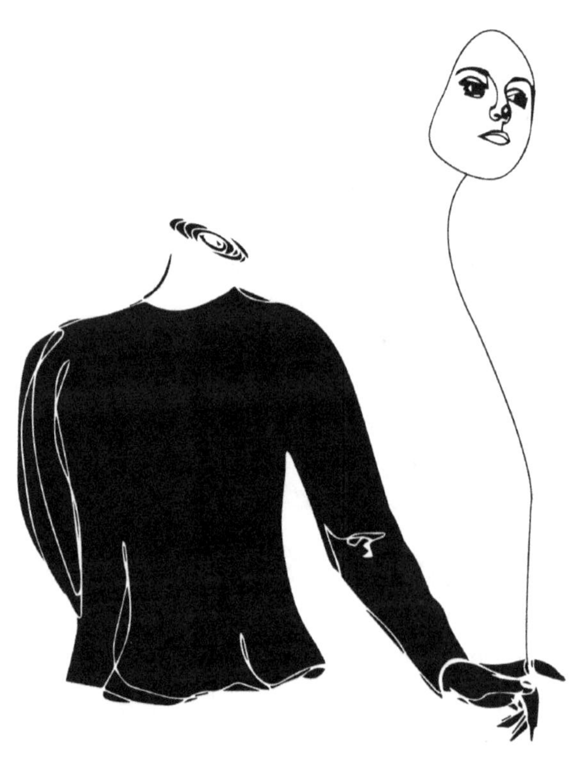

World's Puppet

They tug and pluck at the strings of my mind,
maneuvering me with silky sweet, whispered
suggestions
and feather-light pressure.
("There's only one way to do this thing we call
life.")
They dangle a pair of scissors near me,
just out of reach,
laughing at my clumsy, halfhearted attempts
to grab at them.
("Do you really want to make it?")
When I am close enough to touch them,
close enough to release myself from these
strings,
the cloudy, freezing grip of fear clutches my
heart,
and I cannot do it.
("See? You are nothing when not controlled.")
Sometimes I fight against their pull,
whipping myself around in circles,
hoping to snap the strings.
Sometimes I sag against them.
("Stay with us. You can know peace.")
I couldn't, not really, and I know this.
I know they are lying to me.

But the restraints are tight on my mind,
trapping me in a pounding headache.
("There is nothing more out there for you.")
But there could be, might be,
if I can ever release myself
from the world's never-ending
puppet show.

Those Who Leave

I try my best to cover up
everything you ever gave me.
There's nothing I can do about these
plain brown eyes--contacts aren't for me--
but I can cover every other trace of you,
if I try hard enough.
I pay artists to paint on me in ink,
covering up the freckles you tried to hand down.
I let professionals impale me--my nose, my ears,
my lips--
with metal piercings to disrupt the shape of you
in my face.
I even pay a stylist a hundred dollars every few
weeks,
to chemically change your weak brown hair that
frames my face.
But when I pass by a mirror, I still see you.
You've infiltrated the way I walk,
the way I gesture with my hands
while speaking.
A part of you is in the curve of my hips,
my broad shoulders, my high cheekbones.
When I laugh, I hear your voice,
hear your snort when something is really funny,
feel your tears welling up in my eyes as

I struggle to catch my breath to finish the joke.
My stubbornness is yours, as are my public speaking
skills and my silver-tongued sharp wit.
For someone who was never really there,
you've rubbed a million gifts off on me.
And now, I spend my time running and hiding
from them,
as you've spent your time running and hiding
from me.

The Undead Past

They lurk in the hallways of my mind,
an imprint on the air,
a flash of white around a corner.
I can feel them, even when I
cannot see them, closing in around me,
rifling through drawers of memories,
selecting one and leaving it out for me
to find.
I've apologized and explained,
but nothing will exorcise them.
They guard these memories with
a precious ferocity,
threatening me when I try to discard them,
when I try to shake them off as a dog
shakes off the water after a bath.
They dance and glide inside of me,
making my lungs creak like old floorboards
while I try to sleep at night.
Each morning, I have to rise and
scrape the cobwebs out from my eyes.
They will not let me forget
their names, their faces,
the things we have done to each other.
They understand that memories
keep them alive,

keep them tethered to me in this world.
And I am starting to understand that I am a
person
who is also a haunted house.

Stains of Time

Dead leaves curl around our shoes,
tickling our ankles and whispering softly when
we pass through them.
They are there as a reminder:
time is passing, has passed, will pass.
We don't need them to tell us that.
We have each other as reminders,
our faces a long way off from how they looked
in the elementary school yearbooks.
The fire blazes--a microcosm inferno--in the
metal ring
we all sit around.
Someone pours their solo cup onto the fire
and we all lean back as the sparks fly
like the wishes of dead dandelions in the wind.
We are all remembering the same thing, that
fateful
Bunsen burner in that one science class, ages
ago.
We don't mention it.
We are too young to reminisce and
we don't want to stain this moment,
just in case we want to reminisce on it
in the years to come.

When We Were Happy

We would twirl together,
dancing over the ashes of
our past lovers.
I clutched you like a life preserver,
like the precious diamonds
hanging at my ears that
I'm always so afraid of losing.
Closer, closer, always closer.
What I wouldn't have given to slip
between your ribcage--as if
your ribs were no more than gills--
and to have rested my chest upon your
beating heart.
Memories crumbled and faded beneath
the unforgiving press of our feet.
I would have reached up and pulled the sun
down
from its shelf, if you would've asked,
allowing it to scorch everything that wasn't us.
You, my dear, were something special,
when we were happy.

Traces

Your curls clog my sink
and stick to the sides of my shower walls
like spider legs.
I can see you used my shampoo:
the label isn't turned out, the way I always leave
it.
My hairbrush also holds traces of you,
the handle slick from that vanilla lotion you
love.
Last night, we drank ourselves into oblivion,
lips stinging as we pulled straight from the
bottle,
and filled each other in on our separate lives.
Doesn't it feel strange
that we have two separate lives now?
Ten years ago, we were one.
I can still remember those nights:
two air mattresses, pushed side-by-side
in my parents' living room,
empty chip bags and soda cans littering
the couch behind us, the sun setting
and rising and setting again
as we played video games,
thick as thieves, next to each other.
Today, you left before I woke, no text or note

to say goodbye.
And now I'm left with all these traces of you,
wondering when, exactly, each of us became
an afterthought to the other.

The Parting

Before I step in front of the mirror, I am tall. I
am five feet, eight inches,
and my body has filled out in the way that a
woman's body inevitably does.

My thoughts are heavy, a burden to carry. My
clothes are tight.
I have responsibilities that need attention.

I speak quietly, rarely. On most days, I'm too
tired to be who I am,
so I blend into those around me to avoid
becoming prey.

Every now and then, I find the courage, but
never the situation.
I sink back into my shell before I can be of any
use.

When I step in front of the mirror, a child steps
with me.
I think of how small she is to be wearing that
confident grin.

She wears overalls, and her almost nonexistent
hair has been tied
in the most unattractive tail at the very top of her
head.

Her face is rounded in the way of children, her
cheeks flushed with play.
She reaches out a fat hand to smack the mirror.

I feel myself slipping.

The crash is loud. The mirror is broken.
Mommy will be mad. She'll send me to my
room.

I use my Barbie to push the pieces together.
Then I cover them with my blankie.

I'll tell her the cat did it.

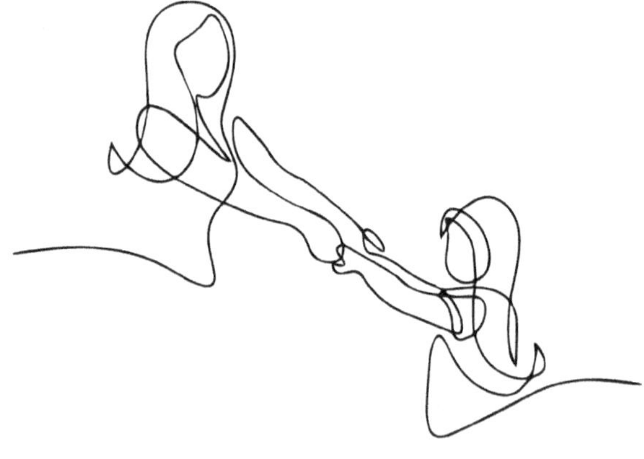

"Good Morning" ("Good Mourning")

I wait in the coffee shop,
the watery morning light scratching
at my hands, my hands that are wrapped around
a paper bag with a bagel inside,
a bag that would be much too loud to open as of
now.
I see you through the window, padding up
the cracked sidewalk, avoiding the leftover piles
of what may have once been snow
but is now lifeless.
I stare down at the table as you approach
because I am too much like those piles out on
the sidewalk and you are the furthest thing from
them.
As you sit, I want to tell you how I revere you in
a way
that borders on sacrilegious, how I worship your
words
and would fall to my knees if you would not
look upon me with scorn for doing so.
But these truths are unutterable, so I pick at
the corner of my paper bag, tear it off, and roll
it between my fingers, hidden under the table.
When I do look up to meet your eyes, I fear

that you have pinned me to my seat
as a collector pins a butterfly to a board,
fear that you have taken my measure--mind and
soul--and have
found me lacking whilst I have been pouring
over you
as a devout pours over biblical passages.
Your eyes are soft, shrewd, curious,
your skin littered with wrinkles and lines
like the bag in my hands--looking at you
reminds me how fleeting this moment could be,
even without me wasting it by only speaking to
you
in my head.
So I gather myself up, creating a dam in my
mind,
a pool for part of me to exist in until I gather the
courage
to release it to you, and say–

An Early Morning With You

The air crackles with life,
sparks like electricity,
when we step out of the car and turn the corner.
It is four in the morning, and the world
is silent, still at peace, lovingly asleep.
The biting April chill surges
with excitement and possibilities,
numbing our fingers and stroking our
sense of anticipation.
We own this street, this world.
It all feels like ours.

The shops are still closed;
the street is partially blocked off by construction,
though even the workers are not awake
at this time.
On the sidewalk, a line of waiters--
not the kind who serve, but the kind like us,
the kind who wait to take--stretches halfway
down the block.
If we were to stop and realize that these waiters
are people too, individuals with a purpose for
being here,
perhaps with the same purpose as us,
we would notice their differences and details:

bundled in blankets, sitting in lawn chairs,
holding books, wrapped in layers,
some chatting quietly, some with the far off gazes
of people who have been camping out here for
hours.
But we do not view them as such.
To us, they are numbers. Obstacles.
Just a data report of how far back in the line we
will be,
how long we will have to wait
before we can enter the shop to take.

We settle onto the sidewalk,
reserving our place, letting the world know
that these squares of sidewalk belong to us.
The fragrance of magic coats the air,
settling deep into our bones, lighting us up.
When I look at you, your eyes are wide in
excitement,
and I can feel the same look in mine,
though I'm not sure where it comes from.
The bricks of the shop behind us cut into
our backs, but we don't mention that to each
other.
We discuss everything else instead.
I know the people on either side of us,
and those crossing in front of us,
seeking their own place to wait,

put you on edge.
I play a game with myself,
seeing how many topics I can bring up
to keep the magic running through your veins.

Hours sprint past us,
but the minutes drag and catch,
getting caught like sandpaper against skin.
We watch the sunrise, watch the lightening of
the sky
behind the beaten-down bars and clubs across
the street.
You don't really drink, aren't very familiar with
these bars,
and I couldn't explain the feel of them to you
even if I wanted to.
But I hope that you can feel the difference,
can feel that those bars don't hold a candle to
the feeling of this morning.

It's not getting warmer, but we don't mention
that either.
You talk like you never have before,
and I bare the parts of myself to you
that I never thought I'd be able to.
Something feels different.
Maybe it's the early morning,
or the lack of light,
or the closeness of knowing somebody

in a crowded line of strangers.
But we are connecting, meshing,
coming together like the sun and the moon
during an eclipse,
blocking out everything else.
And I try not to think of the years wasted,
not feeling like this with you.

We check the time and
rise from our sidewalk guard posts,
treated to the musical cracking of our joints
and the stretch of our muscles.
We are shaking, uncontrollably shaking,
in the cold.
Behind us, the other waiters are growing louder;
their chatter rises to fill the empty street.
It helps us to hear them.
It makes us feel grateful that there are only
sixty people in line ahead of us.
We tell each other that the line will move
quickly,
that next year we'll plan better,
bring warm drinks and wear more layers.
I'm sure that we will, but I don't tell you
that I fear we will never feel like this again.

When our phones read eight o'clock,
the line begins to shuffle forward.
We bounce on our heels,

dipping into the scant line of the morning sun
that is trying to climb over the curb of the street.
I comment on how much warmer I feel in the
sun,
and you laugh like it's the funniest thing
you've ever heard and remind me that
you told me over an hour ago to stand in the sun.

Slowly, our hearts still in the clutches of magic
and
our minds loud with silent pleas of anticipation,
we shuffle forward until
we are at the front of the line.
We peer through the windows,
those dirty windows with the chipped logo
of the vinyl shop painted in the center,
knowing that our hopes are either crushed
or revived based on what we see.
We spot the stack of albums that we came for.
A stack that has surely dwindled during our
wait,
but will have just enough for us.
Still, we fret.

When it is our turn to enter,
we step into the shop quickly,
barely stopping to appreciate the heat
that we have spent the morning begging for.
You lunge to the box of records that you know

has what you are seeking.
A worker, perhaps a waiter--
the kind who serves--
hands you two copies,
and you pass one back to me.
I take it and press it to my chest,
showing you that I value this,
that I will protect this,
though, honestly, I'm not quite sure
which record I am even holding.
I'm not quite sure why we are here,
why we waited this morning.
I just have faith that it means something to you.

With my free hand,
I use my numb fingers to claw through other
boxes,
shifting record sleeves,
searching for someone, or perhaps another
moment,
to jump out at me.
I can feel my nails wanting to break,
wanting to bend.
I stop pawing and searching, but then remember
that we waited for four hours,
and I begin again.

Once we have what we want,
whatever record it is that we came for,

we settle into a calmer excitement.
We can relax now, while still holding onto
our high.
We have what we came for. It is in our grasp.
Nobody can take it from us.
At a slower pace, we meander through the store.
Every now and then, I reach out and collect
something.
After all, the reason we waited was to take.

Before we leave, you check in on me,
make sure I've gotten everything I wanted.
I did not know I wanted anything
before we entered the fervor and life of
this shop around us.
But now I feel that I do.
I whisper the name of an album to you,
and it takes you five seconds to procure it for me
straight from the hands of a worker, waiter.
And it means something to me.
It truly does.
We are both here to make sure the other
gets exactly what they want,
whatever it is,
both here to take care of each other
in every way.

When we leave,
when we step back out onto the sidewalk,

me clutching a large plastic bag
and you delicately holding a brown paper sack
as if it is your child,
it feels like a new day.
We spent only twenty minutes inside,
after four hours of waiting,
but we feel refreshed, invigorated.
The world is once again ours.

The line still stretches down the block
from the shop,
disappearing around the corner and
hiding just how many strangers chose
to have hope today.
We were among them, mere minutes ago.
Now we are above them.
Now we are different.

When we round the corner
and climb back into your car,
I take the keys from you
and feel that everything has changed
in the way that can only happen
when you accept that the world
is truly so small.
I still do not know what is in
my big plastic bag,
still have not peered in to see
which record has sparked so much life in you.

I just trust that this all means something to you,
as it does to me.

You

Sometimes I remember that you used to be
just a face to me, a face with a name that
never interacted with my face, my name.
It feels both like seconds and years now
that we have been sharing this blanket made for
one,
both seconds and years since your roots have
entwined
so deeply inside of me.
It is almost unbelievable that there was a time
when my hand did not know the press of yours,
a time when I did not have the unknowable color
of your eyes memorized.
As I lie next to you in my pajamas, my hair
unbrushed though it is past noon,
I remember the girl who would take two hours
to get ready before meeting with you.
We were young then, weren't we?
We're still young, but I get the feeling that we'll
be doing this for a while: beginning and ending
our days
side by side, creating and absorbing each other,
and sharing this blanket made for one.

Small Talk

I sat on a rock and watched my life from afar
today.
I watched the expressions flit across my face,
heard the edge in my voice,
saw my skin ripple like it might wink from
existence
with or without my consent.
"What do you think?" God asked, pulling up a
lawn chair
next to me.
I shrugged--I have never been one to criticize
another's work--and made a noncommittal reply.
But what I think is that the world could end
and it would feel a lot like this.
Maybe even the rumbling of the world tearing
itself apart would reach my ears,
my ears that refuse to hear so much,
and I would finally understand how it all comes
together:
my body and the world and whatever is lurking
just beneath my skin,
controlling all of this.
Maybe even things would look different and
sound different and smell different.
But it would still feel like this.

"What do you think?" I want to ask.
But do I even care?
Would it even make a difference?
Would it still feel like this?
"The weather's nice," I say instead.
And across the world, I see myself laughing.

To Men, Because You Exist

I will explain. I will
explain
and
explain
and
explain
until it goes away--
that look in your eyes
that pain.
I have been taught to
never waste a word
because it is hard enough to
make
them
listen
in the first place.
I will not be your pet--
not until I have to
not until it comes down to that
and there is
no
other
option.
I will not be your prancing poodle
perfectly tagged and collared

trained at your
beck
and
call.
I will find myself--
someday somewhere,
but not alone
never
on my
own.
I am not safe--
oh how I long to
choose when I want
to
be
safe
and when I want
to
be
free.
If things were different--
if you were different
I would feel the moonlight
on
my
face.
I would smell the lilacs--
that sweet, spring perfume
as they greet me

under
the
stars.
I would smile at strangers
and they would smile back
and strike up a conversation
and I would
listen
and
care.
I would prove myself--
oh but only when I want to,
only by my own regard
and not to
survive
every
day.
I would wear thin dresses--
you know the kind,
the type that flutter
in the breeze
and hand the sunlight
my skin
as
a
gift.
I would admire pretty things--
most of all myself
and not fear who else is

doing
the
same.
I would know Peace
and Freedom and Will--
all close friends.

I fear I'm losing you.
Please, let me explain.
I will explain
and
explain
and
explain

www.ingramcontent.com/pod-product-compliance
Lightning Source LLC
LaVergne TN
LVHW021240200726
843509LV00012B/1542